BEGINNER WORKBOOK

Passion to Profit

STARTING AN ONLINE BUSINESS FROM SCRATCH

Leslie Frank

Table of Contents

Introduction

As online sales grow every year, it's no surprise that more people are starting online businesses. Whether it's a side hustle or a new full-time job, the possibilities are endless. Working from home is easier now than ever thanks to the internet and the multiple platforms available to budding entrepreneurs. You don't need any special degree or certification to start, only an idea and a business plan.

WHO AM I?

You may ask why I have any authority on the subject of online sales. I started my first Etsy business in 2011 after selling casually on eBay for a few years. eBay introduced me to the world of editing listings, talking to customers, and filling orders. I decided to stick with Etsy since it is a better environment for handmade goods. A year later in 2012, I opened my second Etsy shop since the items differed dramatically from what was for sale in my current shop. I was able to quit my day job after a few years thanks to online selling. I expanded my sales into other platforms such as YouTube and Amazon to maximize my profits. I also have experience selling my services through Upwork.

HOW TO USE THIS BOOK

With all these sales and platforms under my belt, I have learned quite a bit about e-commerce. This book contains information from years of trial and error so you can quickly learn from my experiences and avoid some of the mistakes I made. I frequently use the term "shop" but these tips can also be used if you are performing services and don't have an online store. "Shop" can be replaced with terms such as "brand" or "business" to apply to your situation.

In addition to information, this book has many questions and worksheets to help you brainstorm and organize your process. Coming up with a business plan is essential to your success and these worksheets will help organize your thoughts and ideas. Getting your ideas out on paper clears your mind and allows you to see everything at once so you can create a plan of action.

ADDITIONAL RESOURCES

If you find these worksheets helpful, you can also find more organization sheets (both digital and printable) for sale in my Etsy shop at thedigitalcandyshop.etsy.com. I created them for my own personal use and decided to sell them because they were so helpful to me.

For more information on specific platforms, most websites have user guides. Etsy definitely takes the cake with their seller guides. Reading these is essential because they contain information specific to each platform and can help you have more effective listings and a more successful shop.

1

Finding Your Motivation

Before deciding on a product or service to offer, you must decide if you are motivated enough to take on the challenge of starting a business. There are many benefits including:

- A flexible work schedule
- Freedom to sell anything you want
- You don't need any special training or degrees
- Being a beginner is not a disadvantage
- You can easily expand into different platforms
- Be your own boss
- Make money from things you are passionate about

This list is only an overview of the many reasons to jump into self-employment. There are so many types of businesses, industries, and services that you can start immediately, even as a beginner.

WHAT MOTIVATES YOU?

When taking on a business venture, it is crucial to ask yourself why. Your business will not always run smoothly, you will run into bumps along the way, some of which will be very stressful. Having an outline of why you started the business and why you are working so hard can help keep you motivated when things get tough.

Maybe you want to help people by offering a particular service, or maybe you have a product you enjoy making and you'd like to begin selling. You may be doing it solely to make more money and not because you have a particular interest, and that's ok too! Never underestimate the financial incentive, seeing the money roll in is a great motivator.

Find and Keep Motivation

WHAT ARE MY REASONS FOR STARTING AN ONLINE BUSINESS?

WHICH REASON WILL HELP THE MOST DURING STRESSFUL
SITUATIONS?

WHAT OTHER METHODS WILL HELP WHEN I'M FEELING STRESSED?

WHAT IS HOLDING YOU BACK?

In addition to looking at what motivates you, also look at what is potentially holding you back. This is especially important if you have an idea you've been considering but never acted on. Why have you never taken action? It could be as simple as not knowing where to begin or not knowing the platforms, in which case this book will help! It could also be a more personal reason such as being afraid of failure or being afraid of negative feedback. Selling products you create can be especially nerve-wracking when it comes to bad reviews. Figuring out the reason will help you address it and move on.

There is no reason that you can't start an online business, literally anyone can do it with a little research. Look into your fears and what is holding you back. Some of them will be unreasonable, or applicable to anyone. For example, the fear of failure is common to many people and applies to many situations. It is no reason to give up on something.

Another consideration when starting a business is unreasonable expectations. There are many books and articles about online businesses making claims such as "make $10,000 per month," "quit your day job tomorrow," and similar promises. These situations are not normal for anyone starting their own business, although you can work up to them over time. It is unreasonable to believe any of these things, including believing the money will just roll in with very little work. Again, you can work toward this using passive income, but it will not be an immediate return. Make sure you are realistic about your goals and business plan, so you don't get discouraged.

After you determine your fears and unreasonable expectations, you can replace them with reasonable expectations and goals. If your main fear is failure, you can replace it with the reasonable expectation that not every product you offer will be a winner, it's true that some of them will fail. But with this realization, you can set a goal to do market research to find out what sells in your field. This will lessen the chance that multiple items won't sell. The specific goals will depend on your market, but hopefully these examples will help.

Fears and Expectations

WHAT IS KEEPING ME FROM STARTING AN ONLINE BUSINESS?

WHAT ARE MY UNREASONABLE EXPECTATIONS?

WHAT ARE REASONABLE EXPECTATIONS/GOALS TO REPLACE THESE?

2

Starting Out

The first step to starting a business is finding a product or service to offer. You may already have an idea in mind, and this chapter can help finalize your plan. If you don't have an idea, it's time to come up with one!

ONLINE BUSINESS CATEGORIES

There are many categories of online business so you can find what interests you. You may ask which one is the most profitable, but there is no easy answer. There are multiple ways to sell in each category, so it is not one size fits all. The best advice is to pick what interests you so you will stick with it and enjoy it. I made the mistake of jumping into categories I thought would be profitable, only to find out I didn't have enough interest to stick with them. Since I wasn't passionate about making the content, I also didn't make much profit, even though other people found it quite lucrative.

Many categories overlap and work together. Some of the most popular include:

- Advertising
  - This works best combined with other categories such as starting a website or blog so you have a platform that can bring in advertisers. This can be difficult as a stand-alone method since you'll need to bring in many views before it becomes lucrative. For example, if you have a website where you sell advertising space, you need a regular flow of traffic to draw in advertisers. Again this is not quick or easy and is best used after you establish your business and have an audience.
- Blogging
  - Blogging can be a fun venture since you can choose any subject, but again it is not a quick way to make money. It can be a great choice for someone who doesn't want the monetary investment that comes with starting a website, since there are many free blogging platforms. To make money blogging, people generally use advertising and affiliate marketing (more on that later). As previously mentioned, you

will need a decent flow of traffic before this becomes lucrative.

- Starting a website
  - ○ This offers opportunities that blogging doesn't, such as the ability to add e-commerce options and sell products directly from your site. If you are proficient in web design, you can even design websites for other people rather than making money from your own website. This would fall under offering a service. Getting traffic can be difficult and requires research.
- Selling physical products
  - ○ This is how I started out, and how many people gain experience in the beginning. There are countless established platforms to use which makes it easy to jump in without having to set up a website. Some of the more popular platforms include eBay, Etsy, Amazon, Craigslist, and many others. This is one of the quickest ways to make extra money but takes a lot of work if you want to quit your day job.
  - ○ You can create products to sell, or you can resell or "flip" products. Flipping involves purchasing an item then re-selling it for a profit. There may be some labor involved, particularly with flipping furniture, but this can be a great source of income.
- Selling digital products

- This is similar to the previous category, but this involves products that are not physical. Not every platform is friendly to digital content, so be sure to read the guidelines. This can be a source of passive income if you automate the selling process since there is no time spent on order fulfillment. Once you have the product it literally sells itself. E-books fall under this category, but more on those later.

- Offering a service and freelancing
  - You may not have a product to offer, but rather a service. There are endless possibilities including software design, translating documents, creating PDF's, editing in Photoshop, creating illustrations, starting an answering service, being a personal assistant, or anything else!
  - I did freelancing for some time with Upwork and had a great experience, although some people have trouble getting noticed since so many people use the platform. It's best if you can establish yourself as credible before applying to jobs or you may have to take on lower payer jobs in the beginning. I linked to my digital Etsy shop so I could land jobs involving digital product creation like making PDF's or editing photos. If you're lucky/persistent you can find reoccurring jobs that will bring in a steady income.

- Be wary of jobs that sound too good to be true on Upwork, Craigslist, or any platform and don't give away more personal information than is necessary. I got messages almost daily about scam jobs. You can do more research on how to spot a scam but remember that if it sounds too good to be true, it probably is.
- Don't be discouraged by people who low-ball bids on jobs. You will see people bidding as low as $1/hour for jobs that are worth much more, but people will pay more for experience and quality. I had an amazing ongoing job doing Photoshop work and I wasn't the lowest bid, by a long shot. Offer an amount that you think is fair based on your experience and the time needed.

- Affiliate programs
  - Much like advertising, affiliate programs work best if you have an established audience. You link to other products or websites and get a percentage of the sale. You can make a decent amount doing this if you can get enough people to follow you, but remember you don't make anything from clicks, only from sales. This is also not a quick or easy method.
  - Amazon Affiliates is a popular platform but if you don't get enough consistent sales they will cancel your account.

- Writing books
  - This category is one of my more recent ventures, but it's been surprisingly easy thanks to Kindle Direct Publishing. This is Amazon's publishing service which allows you to self-publish books. They automate the process including the printing, so it is a great form of passive income.
  - The main con with this is similar to any category where you make the item you sell. You risk spending time and effort (and perhaps money) to create an item that might not sell.
- Online courses
  - If you have a skill that other people want to learn, this can be a good option. You can make a course on a platform like Skillshare, create an e-book, or make videos on YouTube. You don't necessarily need to be an expert, just a good teacher and knowledgeable about the subject.
- Coaching and consultations
  - This is similar to online courses but may require more knowledge since you will be interacting with people directly. It is a popular option for health and fitness enthusiasts or business analysts.
  - You can combine this with online courses to maximize your income. Offer a broad course in a subject and offer a more personalized consultation

for an additional fee. For example, coach someone on healthy diet habits or analyze their website's user interface.

- Subscription services
  - Another category that pairs well with coaching and online courses is subscription services. You will have to publish content regularly to make it worth it for people to pay for a subscription. Many YouTubers do this through Patreon where you can offer benefits for a monthly fee. You can add tiers for various amounts with different benefits to each tier. You can also use your own website for this service. This works best if you have an established audience or an alternate platform to bring people in.
  - A great example of subscriptions is in the art community on YouTube. Many creators make time-lapse YouTube videos of them creating artwork, then offer a real-time version (generally with commentary) on Patreon for a fee.
- Drop shipping
  - Keeping an inventory of physical products can be a hassle, so some people turn to drop shipping. You don't have to keep the inventory on hand, but rather you contact a supplier to ship the item to the customer directly. The main advantage to this is not worrying about order fulfillment. Unfortunately, this

can also be a disadvantage since you have no control over the quality of the order fulfillment, so you really have to trust your supplier.

- Print on demand
  - If you are into graphic design, print on demand is a good way to offer products you design without having to make the product itself. You can design t-shirts, posters, books, or anything else and have them printed and shipped to order. You don't have to keep an inventory on hand and you only pay a fee for items that sell. Kindle Direct Publishing uses this method for books. The downside is that printing individually can be more expensive than printing in bulk, so there is a smaller profit margin.
- Streaming and video creation
  - YouTube and Twitch are the main platforms for streaming and video creation. Money can be made from advertising, or subscriptions with Twitch. YouTube can be used as your main type of income or as a social media outlet to drive sales. If you want to use YouTube as a stand-alone platform for monetization, you will be making money only from ads. You need to gain a following and meet the criteria before you're able to monetize. This can be a tedious and very difficult process especially since the YouTube search algorithm is making it harder for

small channels to gain subscribers. Even well-established channels recommend having multiple forms of income in case your channel becomes de-monetized.

o I started a YouTube channel for macramé tutorials after I began selling macramé projects on Etsy. After a few months I met the criteria to monetize my video. Many crafters do this to help drive sales and it's fun to make tutorials and help other crafters.

PASSIVE VS ACTIVE INCOME

There are two main types of income for online businesses, passive and active. Passive income is created without you having to do anything since the process is automated. Examples of this include ad revenue, digital products that are automatically shipped, affiliate revenue, or anything where you don't have to actively collect payment and deliver. Passive income requires time to set up in the beginning, but the payoff comes later. The downside is the set up time can be substantial and doesn't always lead to revenue. You may create a product that never sells, or create a YouTube channel for ad revenue that never takes off.

Active income is the opposite, it is collected from a service or an order you have to manually fill. This generally requires less time before you collect payment, although setting up listings and marketing is necessary. You work to fill the order or provide the service after payment is collected, so you are working as you make money. Active income is beneficial in this aspect, but the disadvantage is time. You only have so much time in the day to provide a service or fill orders before you have to outsource. This is something you need to consider when deciding on a product to sell. If you decide to sell quilts, you will only be able to make so many quilts at one time, so your income is limited by your time. Figure out how many of the product you can make in a week and determine your profit to see if it is worth selling.

Business Category Brainstorm

WHAT BUSINESS CATEGORY (OR CATEGORIES) WILL I USE?

WHAT ARE THE PRO'S OF THIS CATEGORY?

WHAT ARE THE CON'S OF THIS CATEGORY?

HOW WILL I ADDRESS THE CON'S?

FIND YOUR NICHE

If you've done any research about selling online, you've probably come across the phrase "find your niche" multiple times. This is because it is an essential part of establishing your customer base. Finding your niche means deciding on a subject for your business, product offerings, or services.

Determining your niche can be a difficult process but I've created a worksheet to help at the end of this section. You will look at your passions, trends, problems that need solving, profitability, and competition. Niches are important for online sales because it will determine the keywords and phrases used in searches. Depending on your platform, you will likely have most of your traffic coming from search. Picking an over-saturated market will bury your website far from page one of the search results. On the other hand, an under-saturated market will have a low number of overall searches. You will need to find a balance.

An unfortunate reality is that niches change. A popular niche can lose popularity and an unpopular niche can suddenly start trending. There is a certain amount of prediction that people use when selecting a niche, and you need to be prepared to change with the times. Think of similar subjects and whether you can transition easily if you need to. Don't put all your eggs in one basket. I started on Etsy selling snarky cross stitch patterns, but that was ten years ago and the market has declined in recent years. At first I just focused on my other Etsy shop, but I later returned and added macramé listings along with tutorials on YouTube to help drive sales, this helped me recover from slowing traffic.

The easiest way to find out the popularity of a niche is to look at what is selling, popular search terms, what is trending, how many items are listed in a category, and prices. I've sold many types of products on Etsy and the first thing I look at is how many items are selling in a category to see how much competition I'll have and the popular prices. Another method I use is looking at what's trending on social media.

If you choose to start a website or blog, you need to look at popular keywords through Google Ads. Not only will you see what people are searching, you can look at profitable keywords to incorporate into your posts to collect ad revenue. Just remember that a higher search volume also means more competition. Similarly, you can also search YouTube for videos related to your subject and look at how many views channels are getting, particularly on recent videos.

Niche Brainstorm

WHAT SUBJECTS AM I INTERESTED IN?

WHAT ARE POPULAR TRENDS SIMILAR TO MY INTERESTS?

WHAT PROBLEMS CAN MY INTERESTS HELP ADDRESS?

Analysis of Competition

HOW MANY OTHER LISTINGS ARE IN MY CATEGORY?

WHAT ARE THE PRICES ON SIMILAR PRODUCTS/SERVICES?

WHAT ARE POPULAR KEYWORDS IN MY SUBJECT?

3

Logo and Branding

After deciding on a niche and type of online business, the next step is creating your brand. Branding is especially important if you use multiple platforms because it will help your audience recognize your content.

The first step of branding is coming up with a name. For some online sellers, they may use their real name. This is appropriate with categories such as freelancing or art, but many people choose to have a shop name or business name. Choosing a name is a daunting task but there are a few tips to make this easier:

- Make the name related to your business category, but not too specific. You want something that makes sense with your shop but you don't want to be locked into a certain category if you change what you sell later. In my first Etsy shop I sold snarky cross stitch patterns. I avoided anything with "cross stitch" in the title since that would lock me into a certain type of item. Eventually I settled on the name "Disorderly Stitches" because it gave me some room to incorporate other fabric and stitching items.

- Make it unique but be careful with alternate spellings. Customers may not remember your alternate spelling and it could cause issues when Googling your business name. Some shops are able to do this though, so use your own judgement here. Just make sure it is something easy to remember but still unique.

- Search your potential name and make sure no other business is already using this. Check with registered trademarks, domain names, Google and any potential platforms such as Etsy and eBay.

- Look at similar businesses to inspire you. Obviously you don't want to steal a name, but looking at names of similar businesses might help you come up with something.

- Make a list of names and ask for opinions. Ask questions such as what they assume you sell, if the name is rememberable, etc. You can ask family and friends but it's best to ask people who don't know anything about your business or what you do. If you already sell, you can ask current customers their opinion.

Business Name Brainstorm

WHAT IS MY BUSINESS CATEGORY?

WHAT WORDS ARE ASSOCIATED WITH MY BUSINESS?

WHAT ARE SIMILAR BUSINESS NAMES?

WHAT ARE POTENTIAL BUSINESS NAMES AND OPINIONS ON THEM?

CREATE A LOGO AND BRAND

After you decide on a business name you can begin creating a logo and other branding elements. Having a consistent brand image is important for an online business so that customers immediately recognize your products or service.

Create a logo or have one professionally designed that you can use across all platforms. You will need it in various sizes to use as thumbnails, avatars, and banners. You can create one yourself if you are good at graphic design, otherwise hire someone to do it. You don't have to invest a fortune, try using a site like Fiverr for a more affordable option. Logo designs vary greatly, you can use an image, text, or a combination of both. Similar to deciding on a name, your logo should make sense for your shop and reflect the kind of products or service you offer. For example you wouldn't want a rustic, traditional logo for a modern graphic design service.

In addition to a logo, you can create a tagline for your business. I'll admit I don't normally use taglines with my businesses since the names are closely related to my products, but it can be a helpful design element to tell people more about your business. If you have a name that doesn't describe what you sell, a tagline may be necessary. A vague name such as "[your name] Designs" would benefit from a tagline describing the type of designs you offer. For example "graphic design at an affordable price" or "interior design on a budget" or "hand-sewn embroidery for the modern woman."

Other designs you want to consider include color scheme and fonts. These will help with recognizability in the same way as a logo and tagline. You don't have to settle on just one font or one color, but rather a family of similar styles. You may use all pastels or all bright colors, or stylized handwritten fonts or type fonts.

Once you know your logo, tagline, font, and color scheme, you can create an email signature and social media sign-off. This is something you can use at the end of posts for your audience to recognize. Depending on the platform, this may be a very short sign-off, or a complex one that includes an image. At the end of a YouTube video you may have an image that include your logo, tagline, name, etc. On the other hand, a twitter post may not have a sign-off at all.

Another element of branding, particularly for handmade shops, small shops, or services includes adding a personal touch. Include your image, a short biography, location, or a short video introducing yourself and your business. On sites such as Etsy, customers like to support small businesses and including a personal touch will make you feel less "corporate." If you offer a service that is completed in person, it will make you more recognizable to your client.

Branding Brainstorm

WHAT ARE DESIGN ELEMENTS I WANT INCLUDED IN MY LOGO?

WHAT ARE COLOR AND FONT FAMILIES I WANT TO USE?

WHAT KEYWORDS DO I WANT TO USE FOR A TAGLINE?

WHAT ARE MY TAGLINE IDEAS?

WHAT WILL I USE FOR AN EMAIL SIGNATURE?

WHAT WILL I USE FOR SOCIAL MEDIA SIGN-OFFS FOR EACH
PLATFORM?

HOW WILL I INCLUDE A PERSONAL TOUCH, WHAT ELEMENTS
WILL I USE?

4

Legal Considerations

Legalities for your business will vary based on your business type and category. Personal preference is also a factor since not everything is mandatory, and some is dependent on your state/country. This section will require research on your own (it is very important to do this!), but it will give you a starting point for what to consider. What makes the tax code so confusing is figuring out what forms, permits, and licenses you need. Once you figure these out, it will become much simpler. The first year of business is the most confusing, but it will get easier I promise!

If you are the only employee in your business, you are considered a sole proprietorship. Luckily this is the easiest business to start since you don't have considerations for other employees which can complicate the process. This classification will be the focus in this book.

It's true that you may not need the following licenses/permits if your sales are low enough, but if you are reading this book then you will probably be making a nice chunk of change with your business, so you'll want to get the legal considerations taken care of as soon as possible so you don't run into problems later. A good rule of thumb is considering whether it's a hobby or a business. If you are just selling an item occasionally and just breaking even on the cost, you'll be fine without a license because it is a hobby. If you are running the business to be as profitable as you can, and you have many sales, definitely look into the following licenses/permits.

MAKE YOUR BUSINESS LEGIT

First, you'll need to get a business license. These licenses vary by state and city, so you'll need to look it up where you live. The hardest part is finding the correct form to fill out, then you pay a small fee and you're all set! You can also register your business with the IRS and get an Employer Identification Number (EIN). The EIN is less important for a sole proprietorship since you can just use your social security number for tax purposes. Another document you may need is a Home Occupation Permit, but this also varies and isn't as common.

Since you will be a profitable business, you'll need to pay taxes on your profits. This is why it is so important to keep records of your income and expenses, so you pay the appropriate amount of taxes. You will not need to pay based on your total sales amount, but rather your profits.

The main forms of taxes in the US are income tax and sales tax. Outside of the US you will pay Value Added Tax (VAT). Make sure you consider how much you'll owe in taxes so you have that amount ready to pay at tax time. If you make enough, you'll have to pay quarterly estimated taxes. This applies if you will owe more than $1000 on your income taxes. The amount you owe can be difficult to estimate especially if it is your first year of business. One of the easiest ways to do this is to keep track of your monthly profits and use an online tax calculator to get an estimate. In future years you can base your estimate on what you owed in the past. You will owe taxes on profits and you may also pay self-employment taxes. These are the taxes that would normally be automatically withdrawn from a pay check such as Medicare and Social Security taxes.

You will also need to track what sales you get within your state so you can pay state sales tax. This process and amount varies by state so you will need to lookup this information for where you live. It's generally pretty easy if you are running an online business because you won't get many sales within your state. This is especially important if you perform services locally or have a local sales venue such as craft fairs or consignment shops.

PROTECT YOUR BRAND AND PROPERTY

This section will cover optional protections for your brand and your intellectual property. There is nothing worse than spending countless hours creating something just to have someone else steal it.

To protect your business name, you can first register it as a "doing business as" name or a DBA. This basically allows you to claim the name for your own use. This process varies by state so you will need to lookup the DBA laws where you live. Usually it is just a fee and protects you for several years. To further protect your brand, you can register trademarks for your name, logo, slogans, etc. This will provide you with protection if someone tries to use it. Filing a trademark is easy but the fees can be steep.

Protecting your intellectual property (anything designed by you) can be accomplished through many different outlets and depends on the kind of material (print vs digital, art vs writing, etc). You may file a trademark or copyright for your designs, although this can get very expensive. Another way is through outlining acceptable use in your terms and conditions or shop policies (more on these later). To make your material less appealing to thieves, make sure you use low-resolution images in previews or use watermarks.

If you design anything online from graphic design to written articles and beyond, you will eventually have someone use your work as their own. I've had this happen several times and I'm sure it will happen again in the future. Luckily most people will fold if you send a cease and desist letter. Tell them the design was created by you and to remove it or legal action will be taken. In all the cases I've encountered they will take the item down.

The choice is yours on what to do next if they don't remove it. You can let it go or contact a lawyer. You will need to prove the design is yours and this is where a trademark or copyright is helpful. You may be able to use less legally-binding forms of proof such as having the design dated before the other person used it (for example, a dated sale or mailing something to yourself), but I advise against relying on this since it may not protect you.

Legal Considerations

WHAT LICENSES OR PERMITS DO I NEED?

WHAT IS THE PROJECTED COST OF THESE LICENSES?

5

Selling your Product/Service

Now that you are an established business, you can begin selling! There are many components of selling online that make it different than selling in person. You need to convey all the information in an easy-to-digest way since you aren't in front of your customer to explain it. Make it easy to read and proofread everything.

HOW TO PRICE YOUR ITEM

Pricing your item or service is always a struggle for the self-employed. You need to price it reasonably, but not so cheap that your profit is too low. There are many calculators to price your items. You'll need to determine your break-even price, wholesale price, and retail price. The break-even price is the exact cost of producing and selling the item without any profit. It is usually the cost of materials plus the cost of labor. Remember to include selling fees in the break-even price. The wholesale price is a bit higher, maybe twice the break-even price, and the retail price is even higher, maybe 3 times the break-even price. The exact formulas for wholesale and retail vary because you will need to consider the market price of your item. The market price is the average amount other people are charging.

The market price is the most important consideration. You can avoid doing any calculations other than break-even and skip to the market price. The reason the break-even cost is so important is because you need to calculate if you're making a profit. There is some wiggle room if you adjust your cost of labor, but make sure the amount is worth your time. One reason I gave up selling most hand-crafted items is because the market price is just too low for the time investment. This isn't true for all handmade items, but it's an important consideration. You don't want to spend time making things that won't sell for a fair price. There is also some wiggle room with pricing passive income products since you will sell many of the same item without any additional expenses.

Pricing Worksheet

PRODUCT:		
TIME:	MATERIALS:	FEES:
SHIPPING COST:	MARKET PRICE:	
BREAK-EVEN:	WHOLESALE:	RETAIL:

Pricing Worksheet

PRODUCT:

TIME:	MATERIALS:	FEES:

SHIPPING COST:	MARKET PRICE:

BREAK-EVEN:	WHOLESALE:	RETAIL:

Pricing Worksheet

PRODUCT:		
TIME:	MATERIALS:	FEES:
SHIPPING COST:	MARKET PRICE:	
BREAK-EVEN:	WHOLESALE:	RETAIL:

Pricing Worksheet

PRODUCT:

TIME:	MATERIALS:	FEES:

SHIPPING COST:	MARKET PRICE:	

BREAK-EVEN:	WHOLESALE:	RETAIL:

Pricing Worksheet

PRODUCT:

TIME:	MATERIALS:	FEES:
SHIPPING COST:	MARKET PRICE:	
BREAK-EVEN:	WHOLESALE:	RETAIL:

Pricing Worksheet

PRODUCT:		
TIME:	MATERIALS:	FEES:
SHIPPING COST:	MARKET PRICE:	
BREAK-EVEN:	WHOLESALE:	RETAIL:

Pricing Worksheet

PRODUCT:		
TIME:	MATERIALS:	FEES:
SHIPPING COST:	MARKET PRICE:	
BREAK-EVEN:	WHOLESALE:	RETAIL:

Pricing Worksheet

PRODUCT:		
TIME:	MATERIALS:	FEES:
SHIPPING COST:	MARKET PRICE:	
BREAK-EVEN:	WHOLESALE:	RETAIL:

ALL ABOUT LISTINGS - PRODUCTS

The listing is as important as the product or service itself. Customers don't have a brick and mortar store to touch your product, so you need to recreate this experience for them. The best way to figure out how to make a listing is to look at listings for similar items. Many of the following points are based on Etsy listings but can easily be applied to any platform including your own website. Ask yourself the following questions:

- In search results, what stands out the most in their listing? What would make me click on it?
- What are common themes in the listing photos for the category? (Indoor/outdoor, what color background, props, closeup/far away, etc?)
- What information is in the tittle?
- What information is included in the description?
- How is the description organized? (Headers, bullet points, etc?)
- Does the product include any customizations or variations?
- What shipping methods are offered?
- What is the price and shipping cost?
- What do I like about this listing?
- What can I improve for my listing?
- What is their competitive edge? What gives me a competitive edge?

If you are selling a product, photos are the most important part of your listing. You'll be surprised by how many people don't read listing descriptions, or even titles. The specifics for how to take photos and what to include will vary based on what you are selling. For small items such as jewelry, many sellers use a light box. These can be bought or made. Larger items have more options but can be more difficult when staging a photo since you'll have to consider what surrounds the item. Before conceptualizing your photo, look into the following technical considerations:

- What is the recommended listing size and orientation?
- What is the recommended resolution? (This is generally 72 PPI for screens.)
- What are the accepted file types? (Usually JPEG is standard, but others may be accepted.)

When you are ready to take your photos, remember the following tips:

- Take a TON of photos from different angles, distances, and lighting setups. You can even try different props and backgrounds. I hate having to re-take photos, so I take dozens to make sure I'll have some winners. You'll want to include all aspects of your item: front, back, top, bottom, inside, outside, in use, not in use, size comparison, closeup, far away, etc. This may seem like overkill but remember you need to re-create the brick and mortar experience.

- Take your photos from far enough away so you can crop them if needed. It is easier to crop than to add extra space around the photo. If you photo is too small, you can always add white space around it, but it is best to just retake it.

- Use natural light whenever possible. If the natural light isn't bright enough, supplement it with artificial white light (as opposed to yellow bulbs). One thing I wish I had invested in sooner is lighting. When I finally folded and bought a halo light for my macramé listings, the images improved dramatically. Again, the type of lighting setup will vary depending on your item.

- Take horizontal images, especially if you use Etsy

- If you use props, keep it simple. You don't want customers to be confused with what they will be receiving. You may want to include a note in your description to clarify. For example, if you are selling journals and the listing photo includes a journal and pen, add a note to the beginning of your listing that states "pen not included."

- Make your photos cohesive by using similar styles, colors, props, etc.

- Consider adding an image with text to explain your listing. As previously mentioned, many people will not read your description (or at least not all of it). One way to clarify important points in your listings is to add an image with a few bullet points. For digital items you can reiterate that it is a digital item and include the file types and programs to use the file. For physical items you may include item specifications or customization options. Make sure the information is concise and easy to read.

You will probably still need to edit the photos, even when adhering to the above tips. Photoshop is my favorite photo editing program, it's the industry standard for a reason, but there are many free options that will be sufficient. You may be able to use the photo editor on your device if you only have minor adjustments to make. I've edited some photos just using my iPad and they look as good as my Photoshop edits!

An alternative to taking photos is to draw them with a program like Illustrator. If you do this, it is a good idea to include a real-life image as one of your listing photos and use the drawn one as the main photo. I have done this many times since I have many digital items. It is a great way to create the photo you want but make sure it is true to the item. Do not embellish it to look different than what the customer will receive.

After you take some killer photos, you'll need to write a title. The listing title should be simple and include keywords to be found in search. The format for your title is based on personal preference and what is common for your item category. I generally include a short descriptive title and maybe a few other specs separated by commas. For example, "Mandala Coloring Book PDF, 60 Pages to Color for Relaxation" or "Small Macramé Wall Hanging, Boho Home Décor, Pink and Navy, Custom Colors Available."

If you are having trouble with the title, try writing your listing tags first. These are short keywords and phrases that will bring people to your listing through search. Pick the tags that best represent your item and combine them into a title. You can also look at other similar listings for title ideas.

The "meat" of your listing is the description. It should be concise, or at least well-organized, with the most important information at the beginning. If you have a lot of information, separate it with headers and use dashes as bullet points. For some platforms such as Kindle Direct Publishing, you can use HTML in your listing. Make sure you preview the finished listing if you use HTML to check that everything is showing up correctly.

The information included in your description can include the item specifications, important policy information (more on shop policies later), shipping times and methods, uses for your item, contact information, and any important points you feel are crucial to your item. You don't need to add all of these points, and you shouldn't add anything that isn't necessary. For example, most platforms include a button to message you, so you probably don't need to add contact information unless your item includes customizations. Then you can point out how to contact you.

Listing Worksheet

PRODUCT:	
COMPETITIVE EDGE IN OTHER SHOPS :	MY COMPETITIVE EDGE:
PRODUCT SIZE AND MATERIALS:	
TAGS:	
TITLE:	
DESCRIPTION BRAINSTORM:	
CUSTOMIZATIONS:	SHIPPING OPTIONS:
NOTES:	

Listing Worksheet

PRODUCT:	
COMPETITIVE EDGE IN OTHER SHOPS:	MY COMPETITIVE EDGE:
PRODUCT SIZE AND MATERIALS:	
TAGS:	
TITLE:	
DESCRIPTION BRAINSTORM:	
CUSTOMIZATIONS:	SHIPPING OPTIONS:
NOTES:	

Listing Worksheet

PRODUCT:

COMPETITIVE EDGE IN OTHER SHOPS :	MY COMPETITIVE EDGE:

PRODUCT SIZE AND MATERIALS:

TAGS:

TITLE:

DESCRIPTION BRAINSTORM:

CUSTOMIZATIONS:	SHIPPING OPTIONS:

NOTES:

Listing Worksheet

PRODUCT:	
COMPETITIVE EDGE IN OTHER SHOPS :	MY COMPETITIVE EDGE:
PRODUCT SIZE AND MATERIALS:	
TAGS:	
TITLE:	
DESCRIPTION BRAINSTORM:	
CUSTOMIZATIONS:	SHIPPING OPTIONS:
NOTES:	

Listing Worksheet

PRODUCT:	
COMPETITIVE EDGE IN OTHER SHOPS :	MY COMPETITIVE EDGE:
PRODUCT SIZE AND MATERIALS:	
TAGS:	
TITLE:	
DESCRIPTION BRAINSTORM:	
CUSTOMIZATIONS	SHIPPING OPTIONS:
NOTES:	

Listing Worksheet

PRODUCT:

COMPETITIVE EDGE IN OTHER SHOPS:	MY COMPETITIVE EDGE:

PRODUCT SIZE AND MATERIALS:

TAGS:

TITLE:

DESCRIPTION BRAINSTORM:

CUSTOMIZATIONS:	SHIPPING OPTIONS:

NOTES:

Listing Worksheet

PRODUCT:	
COMPETITIVE EDGE IN OTHER SHOPS :	MY COMPETITIVE EDGE:
PRODUCT SIZE AND MATERIALS:	
TAGS:	
TITLE:	
DESCRIPTION BRAINSTORM:	
CUSTOMIZATIONS:	SHIPPING OPTIONS:
NOTES:	

Listing Worksheet

PRODUCT:

COMPETITIVE EDGE IN OTHER SHOPS:	MY COMPETITIVE EDGE:

PRODUCT SIZE AND MATERIALS:

TAGS:

TITLE:

DESCRIPTION BRAINSTORM:

CUSTOMIZATIONS:	SHIPPING OPTIONS:

NOTES:

Listing Worksheet

PRODUCT:	
COMPETITIVE EDGE IN OTHER SHOPS:	**MY COMPETITIVE EDGE:**
PRODUCT SIZE AND MATERIALS:	
TAGS:	
TITLE:	
DESCRIPTION BRAINSTORM:	
CUSTOMIZATIONS:	**SHIPPING OPTIONS:**
NOTES:	

Listing Worksheet

PRODUCT:	
COMPETITIVE EDGE IN OTHER SHOPS :	MY COMPETITIVE EDGE:
PRODUCT SIZE AND MATERIALS:	
TAGS:	
TITLE:	
DESCRIPTION BRAINSTORM:	
CUSTOMIZATIONS:	SHIPPING OPTIONS:
NOTES:	

Listing Worksheet

PRODUCT:

COMPETITIVE EDGE IN OTHER SHOPS :	MY COMPETITIVE EDGE:

PRODUCT SIZE AND MATERIALS:

TAGS:

TITLE:

DESCRIPTION BRAINSTORM:

CUSTOMIZATIONS:	SHIPPING OPTIONS:

NOTES:

ALL ABOUT LISTINGS - SERVICES

If you are providing a service, clients won't be talking to you in person. In most cases they won't even hear your voice, at least when deciding whether to hire you. You will need to express your professionalism and trustworthiness through your listing. I suggest reading through the above product listing advice since most of it can be applied. The following points are based on creating an Upwork profile but can be applied to any platform including your own website.

- Use a professional profile picture. You don't have to pay for one, but look professional, smile, and use a simple background. Similar to the listing photo considerations, use natural light and make sure the size and format are correct.

- Make an intro video. Many platforms allow you to create a short video to introduce yourself. This isn't necessary, and it's not something I did personally, but if you are relying solely on freelance work then it's probably a good idea. Make sure your video is professional and write a script so you know exactly what to say. Explain who you are, your qualifications, the type of work you do, and what jobs you are interested in. Watch other freelancer's videos to help figure out what to include or leave out.

- In your introduction, highlight why you are the best choice for your field. List certifications and notable jobs.

- Include mockups and previous work, as well as employment history. You can also link to other accounts such as LinkedIn.
- Proofread, then proofread again!
- Be concise but informative and complete all sections in your profile. Be professional but not generic, give it a personal touch.

Freelance Intro Worksheet

COMPETITIVE EDGE OTHERS HAVE:	MY COMPETITIVE EDGE:

CATEGORIES FOR MY SERVICES

MY CERTIFICATIONS:

NOTABLE JOBS:

INTRODUCTION OUTLINE:

NOTES:

Freelance Intro Worksheet

COMPETITIVE EDGE OTHERS HAVE:	MY COMPETITIVE EDGE:

CATEGORIES FOR MY SERVICES

MY CERTIFICATIONS:

NOTABLE JOBS:

INTRODUCTION OUTLINE:

NOTES:

Policies and Customer Service

The best way to avoid problems in your shop is to outline your policies clearly. Policy considerations are different depending on if you have physical products, digital products, or services. Policies are important because it will let your customers know what to expect and give them a good idea of how you handle customer service. You want to be clear and friendly. Many platforms have a space for policies and some sellers list them in their item descriptions.

Information for your policies may include:

- A short welcome note including contact information

- Payment information including a statement that items are not shipped/made until payment is cleared
- Shipping information including methods and shipping times
- Refund and exchange policy. This is an important point to include and you may want to add it to your item descriptions especially for digital items. Most shops do not offer refunds on digital items, so it is important to include this in your description. Some shops will charge a "restocking fee" for costs that can't be recovered. This can dissuade customers so only include it if you feel it's absolutely necessary. Be upfront with your refund policy. Include who will pay return shipping and if original shipping will be refunded.
- Digital item use policy. This section can be extensive because it covers all the uses and non-uses for digital items.
- Frequently asked questions (FAQ) section and troubleshooting
- Make sure you proofread your policies
- Include a note to contact you for clarification

Any order problems should be addressed on a case-by-case basis and leniency is the best policy. Protect your reviews and make good customer service a priority. I have many repeat customers and I credit this to my customer service. The following are examples of some problems and how to address them:

- Problems using a digital file

- 99% of the time this is due to the app or device and not the file. Suggest steps such as deleting and downloading everything again, restarting the device, updating the app, etc. Google is your friend. As much as you may want to tell the customer to Google it themselves, just do it yourself and give them some options.
  - If there is a problem with the file, correct it or refund the order.
- Customer mistakenly bought a digital item
  - If the customer thought they were receiving a physical item, you have a few options. In many cases you can see if they downloaded the item. If it hasn't been downloaded, give a refund. If the item has been downloaded, you can decide how to proceed. Let them know that you do not offer refunds on digital items that have been downloaded and apologize. You can offer a refund if they keep pushing, it's up to you.
  - If this happens often, add something to your listing image explaining that the item is digital. Also add a note to your description such as "Please note this item is digital, you will not receive a physical item."
- Problems due to customer not reading the description
  - Offer a partial or full refund
  - Offer a replacement or exchange

- Explain to the customer the timeline for their choice. For example, you will not ship the replacement until their item is shipped back to you, or they will not receive a refund until you receive the item.
- Tell the customer if there is a time limit such as shipping the item back within a month.
- Decide who will pay return shipping, hopefully this is outlined in your shop policies.
- Update your listing and photos to be clearer, especially if this happens more than once.
- You can choose to do nothing, but you risk a bad review.
- Item was damaged
  - Offer a partial or full refund
  - Offer a replacement or exchange
  - Explain to the customer the timeline for their choice. For example, you will not ship the replacement until their item is shipped back to you, or they will not receive a refund until you receive the item.
  - Tell the customer if there is a time limit such as shipping the item back within a month.
  - Decide who will pay return shipping, hopefully this is outlined in your shop policies.
- Customer did not like item
  - Offer a partial or full refund
  - Offer a replacement or exchange

- Tell the customer if there is a time limit such as shipping the item back within a month.
- Decide who will pay return shipping, hopefully this is outlined in your shop policies.
- You could also choose to do nothing but expect a bad review

- Item was not as described, or other problems that are your fault
  - Offer a partial or full refund
  - Offer a replacement or exchange
  - You should be the most lenient with this case since it was your fault. Make sure you update the listing to be clearer and thank the customer for pointing out the problem.
  - Offer to pay for return shipping. You will likely be eating the cost in this situation, but it will protect your reviews and likely still get you a good review from the customer since you are working with them.

You may wonder if lenient return policies will lead to you losing money, but if you focus on being clear and providing good customer service, your shop will rarely have problems. Learn from your mistakes if you do have a return.

SPECIAL CONSIDERATIONS FOR SERVICES

Outlining policies for services, freelance work, and custom work is essential for avoiding problems. Make sure all aspects of the order are clearly outlined in the beginning so the client isn't unhappy with the finished product. When pricing your service, consider the revisions or additional work you'll need to do. You may need to include specific revisions in your pricing and the cost of additional ones, or you can price your service with the expectation that you will be doing revisions or extra work.

When I created PDF's on Upwork, I chose the latter. I knew there would be changes to the file and layout and included this in my price. A better way to do this is charging a per hour cost instead of a flat cost, this way you know you will be paid for your time. If a client isn't happy with your work, it is your responsibility to fix it, even if you eat some of the costs.

ADDRESSING A BAD REVIEW

What happens when you get a bad review? The first step is not to panic! It can be disheartening to see a bad review, but there is time to change it. Avoid responding to it publicly at first since this usually prevents the customer from changing their review. Contact the customer and address what was in the review. Try to fix the problem. Usually if you fix the problem, they will update their review. If you do fix the problem and they seem happy but do not update their review, ask them nicely if they would consider updating it if they are satisfied and to let you know what else you can do if they are still unhappy.

You may end up with a bad review that sticks. In this case you can respond to it publicly. I have one 1-star review on Etsy from a few years ago when I sold planners. I had an order that was delayed due to an unforeseen circumstance. I contacted the customer about the delay, but when the updated shipping date arrived, I still wasn't able to complete the order so I cancelled it. This was a month-long ordeal (planners normally took up to 2 weeks to ship), so the customer was understandably annoyed.

I gave a full refund and apologized but that didn't make up for the ordeal. She left a 1-star review after I gave the refund. I responded to it stating that I gave a full refund and it was due to an unforeseen circumstance and unrepresentative of my shop. I stopped selling planners at this same time so it's hard to say if it affected my sales. It didn't seem to affect my other items and it wasn't long before it was buried behind many 5-star reviews.

People generally understand that problems will occur and there are very few shops that don't have at least one negative or neutral review. The customer's concern is usually how recently it occurred, your response, and how often it happens.

Shop Policies Outline

RETURN AND EXCHANGE POLICY:

SHIPPING POLICY:

OTHER POLICIES:

OTHER POLICIES (CONT.)

Potential Problems and Solutions

PROBLEM:	HOW I WILL ADDRESS IT:
PROBLEM:	HOW I WILL ADDRESS IT:
PROBLEM:	HOW I WILL ADDRESS IT:

Potential Problems and Solutions

PROBLEM:	HOW I WILL ADDRESS IT:
PROBLEM:	HOW I WILL ADDRESS IT:
PROBLEM:	HOW I WILL ADDRESS IT:

Potential Problems and Solutions

PROBLEM:	HOW I WILL ADDRESS IT:
PROBLEM:	HOW I WILL ADDRESS IT:
PROBLEM:	HOW I WILL ADDRESS IT:

7

Managing your Business

After you get your shop setup, your next step is to manage your business. This step will be ongoing for as long as you stay open. Managing your business is an exciting and daunting task, but can be made easier with a few pointers.

ORGANIZATION AND AUTOMATION

You only have so much time in the day to devote to your shop. Whatever the method, you need to get organized and automate as many steps as possible. Some tasks that can be automated include:

- Social media posts, including YouTube videos
- Email campaigns

- Scheduling sales and coupons
- Shipping digital items
- Sending invoices and tracking updates
- Inventory management
- Some tax information and sales records
- Follow up email to remind customers to leave feedback
- Bill payments
- Some parts of product design such as book covers, digital paper, or even hiring a ghost writer for books.

For tasks that can't be automated, create a checklist of steps. For example, if you create a product to order, have a checklist for each step of creating the product so you don't skip anything. Make the final step "ship item." When you have many orders to ship, it can be easy to skip a step or forget to ship something. Consider making the checklist look nice and match your shop branding, then include it in the package to show your commitment to quality.

Another consideration is the organization of your workspace. Even if you are a messy person (like me), devote one area of your house to be a workspace. This can be beneficial during tax time because you may qualify for a home office deduction, but it can also help keep you organized. Have your materials lined up in order of how you need them. This may seem unnecessary, but when you have dozens of orders open at one time, it will keep you from having to run around finding everything you need. For example, if you are packaging a journaling kit, you may have your materials lined up from left to right as follows:

- Journal
- Pen
- Stickers
- Cellophane bags
- Box and packaging materials
- Printer for shipping label

This concept can also be applied to services that you perform online. When I did Upwork I organized my computer taskbar to reflect the programs I needed for jobs. I had the Upwork app, Documents, Photoshop, Illustrator, Acrobat, and a web browser (with an organized bookmarks toolbar) lined up for easy access. It was so easy for me to get started working because I didn't have to think about what programs or windows I needed open, I just clicked through everything.

ALWAYS BE EXPANDING

Even if your business is a side hustle, you should always be focused on expanding. This may include adding more items, or exploring new platforms. The best way to decide how to expand involves looking at what is selling the most and what customers are asking about. You will get questions about products or customizations that you may not be interested in, but if you get many similar requests you should consider adding that item to your store. Similarly, if you get requests for a service, it may be worth learning a new skill.

Using a new platform can be a bit more intimidating, but it gets easier with each new one you add. Look into platforms with minimal starting costs and something similar to what you already do. Don't forget to look at new platforms that might be trending.

WHEN YOU FEEL OVERWHELMED

A few years ago when Etsy was only a side hustle, I had a greeting card featured on Buzzfeed just before Thanksgiving. I went from selling 10-20 cards per week to selling around 150 over a weekend! I was ecstatic but also terrified because I had no idea how to handle that many sales. I had to make an emergency materials run and work around my day job schedule, but I pulled through after a few incredibly overwhelming days.

You may be overwhelmed for any number of reasons, but there are some tips to help you keep sane. Remember that the worst case scenario is that you cancel a few sales or contact some customers about shipping their order late. During my greeting card extravaganza, I had to ship some of the orders late. I contacted the customers and they were all very understanding. No orders had to be refunded and all of my reviews were fantastic. People will usually work with you if you let them know what's happening.

Another option is outsourcing tasks. If this is a long-term problem, outsourcing or automation might be necessary. You could also try raising the price to make up for those late nights filling orders. Remember supply and demand, if demand is high then you can balance it by adjusting your price. In some cases, you may have to say no, especially with custom orders. I rarely take custom orders because I don't have the time. Don't feel pressured to take custom orders if it makes you feel overwhelmed.

Management Worksheet

WHERE DO I STRUGGLE WITH EFFICIENCY?

WHERE AM I FEELING OVERWHELMED?

WHAT TASKS CAN BE AUTOMATED?

8

Marketing and Driving Sales

Perfect items, listings, and policies don't matter unless customers actually see your shop and listings. Fortunately, most selling platforms will bring in views from search, but you can maximize your sales through marketing.

WAYS TO MARKET YOUR SHOP

- Sponsored Listings
  - Platforms such as eBay and Etsy allow you to purchase sponsored listings. This is a good way to get more views, but make sure you're making more in sales than you're paying.

- Other Ads
  - Google AdSense is a popular way to advertise, but there is a learning curve. You will need to do research on keywords and create ads for Google to run. This is a good option for advertising websites or blogs.
  - Social media outlets also offer advertising opportunities. Instagram and Facebook are great for small businesses.
- Affiliate Marketing
  - This was previously mentioned as a way to make money, but it can also be a way to collect sales. You can pay others a percentage for each sale they bring to you.
- Email Marketing
  - If you already have an established audience, you can use email marketing to bring people to your shop. You can let them know when you have new items and sales.
  - You can offer an incentive such as a coupon code for signing up
- Guest Blog
  - Contact popular blogs in your market to write a guest blog post to bring people to your shop. Tell them why you are a good fit and offer a benefit for them such as a free product or giveaway.

- Look at their posts and comments to see if they have an engaged audience.
- Put your logo and link on everything
  - Shipping labels, stickers on merchandise, business cards, email signatures, and everything else should have your logo and link. You can even advertise via stickers on your car!
- Comment on forums and posts
  - Add helpful comments to forums, social media posts, YouTube videos, and everywhere else! Include you link in your signature on forums and on your social media profiles
  - Don't spam.
- SEO (Search Engine Optimization)
  - Everything you post should include keywords for search engines to recognize. Make sure these aren't too forced, especially on social media. You don't want to overdo it. Keyword dumping can harm you because it looks like spam.
- Call to Action
  - Include calls to action in your posts and emails. Tell people to like, subscribe, favorite, and visit your shop and social media.
  - If you watch YouTube you'll notice most people saying to like and subscribe at some point in their video, this is because it works!

OTHER FACTORS TO DRIVE SALES

- Visual Appeal
  - Make sure your logos, listings, etc are visually pleasing and consistent. Appearance is everything when selling online
- Sales
  - Have sales to encourage people to try your products
  - Make sure you run sales during popular times of the year such as black Friday, back to school, etc.
- Giveaways
  - Social media giveaways are a great way to get your name out there and bring in views. Entries for the giveaway can include sharing a post and commenting.
- Social Media Presence
  - Even if you don't post often on social media, have your information available if someone searches for you. Link to your shop, website, etc.
- Start a blog
  - This can be time consuming if it isn't your focus, but starting a blog provides both marketing and engagement opportunities, similar to social media. This is a good way to get sign-ups for an email list.
- Have a consistent routine
  - Develop a posting schedule for social media so your audience knows when to expect new content.

- Post new items regularly
- Complete all parts of your selling profile
    - Every platform has sections for a profile such as logo, location, intro, etc. Fill out all the information so your profile is complete.
    - If you have a website make an "About me" page, be sure to include social media links and a link to your shop.
- Protect your reviews
    - This can't be overstated.
- Be mobile-friendly
    - Check your selling platforms, social media, blog, or website to see how it looks on phones and tablets.
- Offer free shipping
    - Even if you include the shipping cost in your item, the appearance of free shipping can encourage sales.
    - Make sure the final price is close to the market price if you choose to include shipping in the list price. If shipping is especially expensive, it may be a good idea to list the shipping cost separate. You can experiment with both methods and see what works for you.
- Offer incentives
    - Coupon codes, BOGO deals, sales, giveaways
- Generous return policies

o   If you are confident in your product, having generous return policies will help because people will be more willing to try your products.

Marketing Worksheet

WHAT ARE THE BEST WAYS TO MARKET MY SHOP?

WHAT FREE METHODS WILL I USE TO DRIVE SALES?

9

Analyzing Your Strategy

When selling online there are many expenses to consider, so you need to keep records to check whether you are making a profit. No matter what your profit is, you should always be analyzing your sales strategy to maximize your income.

You can use many different methods to keep records, both physical and digital. I offer business planners on Etsy and Amazon, or there are programs you can use to keep track of your numbers. What numbers should you be tracking? Everything! Track your social media following, your views, your sales, your total income, expenses, etc. Find out what is normal for your shop so you can try new strategies. Keep track of when you test a new strategy and see how it affects your sales.

Looking at which items sell the most can help you come up with new related items or variations. Similarly, looking at which social media posts get the most views, likes, and shares can help you create posts that will have repeated success. You'll be surprised at how much these stats and sales will improve if you start monitoring and repeating what works for your shop.

I'll admit I wasn't good at tracking these stats a few years ago, but once I began setting goals and monitoring them, I started selling more items. Just the process of goal setting seemed to increase my sales and gave me motivation to keep creating products and expanding my sales outlets. It can be really encouraging.

Of course, it could work the other way and you could find that you aren't getting nearly as many sales as you thought, or that your profits are much lower than your sales would suggest. Don't be discouraged by this, see it as a learning opportunity. Find exactly why your expenses are so high or where you can improve and see if the changes help.

CHANGE WITH THE TIMES

One downside of having a well-established shop is coming to the realization that it will become outdated, it's just a matter of time. This is easy to address with a few changes. I recently discovered that in order to increase my Etsy sales, I might not need more items, but rather a revision of my item listings. Some of my previously listed items were looking dated. The colors, fonts, and styles just weren't working anymore. Instead of creating new items from scratch, I revised the listing photos and updated the tags and it wasn't long before they were getting more views.

Another problem with the changing times is that trends change and items that previously sold will lost popularity. The upside is that the opposite can happen too. This is why it's helpful to have different platforms and different types of related items. On the other hand, sometimes changing the listing photo isn't enough and you need to change the product or simply add more products to your shop. Remember that quantity isn't always better and don't be afraid to remove listings that aren't selling.

Shop Analysis

WHAT ITEMS AREN'T SELLING?

WHAT PROBLEMS DO I SEE WITH THESE ITEMS OR LISTINGS?

HOW CAN I CHANGE THE ITEM OR LISTING?

Successful Listings Stats:
Year 20___

MOST PURCHASED LISTINGS:

MOST REVENUE LISTINGS:

MOST VIEWED LISTINGS:

Successful Listings Stats: Year 20__

MOST PURCHASED LISTINGS:

MOST REVENUE LISTINGS:

MOST VIEWED LISTINGS:

Successful Listings Stats:
Year 20__

MOST PURCHASED LISTINGS:

MOST REVENUE LISTINGS:

MOST VIEWED LISTINGS:

10

Do's and Don't's

DO PAY YOURSELF FOR YOUR TIME

Make sure you pay yourself enough to keep you motivated. The amount you pay yourself is subjective and you don't necessarily have to use an hourly wage, just make sure the total amount is a number you're comfortable with. If you price your time too low, every order will feel like a chore because you aren't valuing your time.

DO HAVE LENIENT POLICIES

You need to have all of your policies laid out clearly but be willing to bend if the situation calls for it. This is part of providing excellent customer service.

DO USE MANY PLATFORMS

Don't put all your eggs in one basket. You don't have to be the best on one platform if you can be moderately good on many platforms. Look at the total amount of profit you make rather than how good you are on a specific platform.

DO ANSWER QUESTIONS POLITELY AND TIMELY

I've mentioned several times how important it is to provide good customer service, and this is another requirement for selling online. Always protect your reviews.

DO FOLLOW PLATFORM RULES, EVEN IF OTHERS DO NOT

You may be discouraged by the number of resellers you see on Etsy who claim their item is handmade when it isn't, or by the number of copyright/trademark infringements, but always follow the rules of the platform. Ignorance is no excuse, so educate yourself.

DO EVALUATE YOUR PRODUCTS CRITICALLY

Always look at your products or services as if you are the buyer. Would you buy your product or hire yourself for a service? Why or why not? If not, improve your product by examining why you wouldn't buy it. You can also ask friends, family, or former customers for ways to improve.

DO COMPLETE YOUR PROFILE

Complete all fields in listings and on your profile, it will make you look more professional and show your attention to detail.

DO KEEP UP WITH CHANGING POLICIES AND FEES

Platforms are always changing their policies, fees, and terms and conditions. Sometimes they will email you about updates, but make sure you investigate on your own.

DO BE DETAILED BUT CONCISE

Include all necessary information in your listings but make it as concise as possible. If you have a lot of information to include, use headers, dashes, or bullet points to organize it and put the most important information at the beginning. Also consider including text in your listing photos.

DO MARKET RESEARCH

This is one of the most important steps in your process because it can help you determine how much money you will make. Look at what items sell, how others list them, what their photos look like, the average selling price, and any other relevant information. If you provide a service, look at the average amount per hour, what certifications other people have, their past jobs, etc.

DO PACKAGE ITEMS CAREFULLY

Don't let your hard work be destroyed by skimping on packaging. Make sure you use sturdy shipping materials and peanuts or void fill bags whenever needed.

DO YOUR BEST WORK ALWAYS

It's easy to lose commitment over time, especially when the process become monotonous, but remember to commit to quality with every order. Each order is a new customer who is likely seeing your work for the first time, make sure it's always a good experience.

DON'T SACRIFICE QUALITY

If you choose to outsource or you are trying to cut your expenses, make sure you don't sacrifice quality. The only time this might work is if you make the price point low enough to fit the customer's expectation. Some customers are willing to pay less for a lower quality item.

DON'T DELAY ORDERS WITHOUT COMMUNICATION

Most people are understanding if you are up front with them about any problems or delays. Don't hesitate to contact them if there is a problem. Tell them about the delay (don't get too personal), when they can expect it, and offer a refund if they don't want to wait. If you don't hear back from them, assume they are ok with waiting. The whole message should only be a few sentences. An example message is: "Thank you for your order! Due to an unforeseen circumstance, I will not be able to ship your order by [Monday] as estimated, I will have it shipped on [Thursday] instead. Sorry for any inconvenience. If you don't want to wait, I can provide a full refund, otherwise I will ship it on [Thursday]. Thank you for understanding!"

DON'T WORK FOR FREE

If you are a creative person, your friends and family have likely asked you do something for free. You can decide if you're comfortable with it, but otherwise you should charge for any service you provide because your time is valuable. Only work for free if there is a benefit for you such as expanding your portfolio or gaining experience.

DON'T HAVE UNREASONABLE EXPECTATIONS

Your expectations have a significant impact on your self-esteem in any situation. Make sure you have reasonable goals and expectations for your business.

DON'T OBSESS OVER NUMBER OF SALES

The total number of sales doesn't mean anything other than bragging rights. You should always focus on profit. There are shops with thousands of sales but may only make a very small profit from each sale, but it works the other way also.

DON'T FEEL PRESSURED TO HAVE DISCOUNTS

Many shops offer discounts for bulk purchases or buying multiple items but use these at your discretion. I like to price my items low and use discounts sparingly, but every shop is different, so test which works better for you. One discount I do use is the abandoned cart discount and I run sales during certain times of the year like Christmas and back to school.

DON'T USE ADS IF THEY DON'T PROVIDE A RETURN

Ads don't automatically bring a return, so monitor them closely to see if they work. Etsy and KDP make this easy but other platforms may require more work. When you look at the total sales from ads, make sure you subtract expenses and fees from the total sales to make sure you aren't losing money. You can always take a break from ads and try again later. If you're able to choose keywords like on AdSense or KDP, try using different phrases.

DON'T BE RUDE

If you get questions that have an obvious answer or you have a rude customer, it's easy to get annoyed. Take a minute to gather your thoughts and come back to the message so your gut reaction can dissipate, then you can respond with a clear head. Some platforms allow you to have a draft saved for common questions. If you get the same question repeatedly you may want to change the listing or add a short FAQ to the description.

DON'T SPAM

Spam comes in many forms, none of which you should engage in. Don't spam on forums or in comments, and don't spam convos if a person asks about a custom item.

DON'T COMPROMISE ON LISTING PHOTO QUALITY

You may be excited to post a listing, only to find out your photos don't look so great. Not bad, but not listing-worthy. In this case it's best to wait until you have better photos otherwise your views will suffer, and possibly your shop's integrity. Only post your best work and photos are such a valuable part of your listing. A fantastic description will not make up for poor photos.

DON'T COPY, LIE, OR RESELL (UNLESS ALLOWED)

Never copy another person's work or lie about your work. Don't imply that you created a pattern yourself if you didn't and always give credit where it's due. Reselling is a gray area because it depends on the platform. Don't resell a mass produced item while claiming (or implying) it is handmade.

DON'T IMMEDIATELY RESPOND PUBLICLY TO A BAD REVIEW

You may be antsy to respond publicly to a bad review to set the record straight, but it's better to wait and contact the person directly. In many cases, responding publicly will make it unable for the person to change their review. If you contact the person and it's clear they will not allow you to fix the problem and update the review, then you can respond. Make sure your response is professional and avoid blame and name-calling.

I hope you've found the information in this book helpful and you are ready to start selling! Taking the jump to being self-employed can be scary, so prepare yourself by doing as much research as possible and doing the best work you can. Once you get your feet off the ground it can be very exciting because the possibilities are endless!

Leave a Review

THANK YOU FOR READING AND LET ME KNOW IF YOU LIKED THE BOOK!

Print More Worksheets

FIND PRINTABLE VERSIONS OF THE WORKSHEETS IN THIS BOOK AT:

https://drive.google.com/open?id=1ezVgmREpzitDgVriC6eNH8KZTNP1o9B9

Beyond this Book

FIND MORE WORKSHEETS AT MY ETSY SHOP THEDIGITALCANDYSHOP.ETSY.COM AND A BUSINESS PLANNER ON MY AUTHOR PAGE ON AMAZON

Printed in Great Britain
by Amazon